Incorrect Rhymes

The Ultimate Challenge

Be Inspired

Elma Burke, Janvier Burke and Janeal Burke

Illustrated by Ariane Motondo

Library of Congress Control Number: 2018905852
ISBN: Softcover   978-1-5434-9032-9
               eBook   978-1-5434-9031-2

Print information available on the last page.

Rev. date: 06/07/2018

To order additional copies of this book, contact:
Xlibris
800-056-3182
www.Xlibrispublishing.co.uk
Orders@Xlibrispublishing.co.uk
776028

Dedication

To the awesome boys in my life, thank you for being my inspiration from the very first poem "Ice Age" to the last poem "Mosquito". Janvier and Janeal the world is your oyster. Let challenges become victories and your stories become books.

There is a book in you
There is a book in me
If we keep on writing
Then a book we shall see

To all the wonderful children I have worked with and will work with in the future, "keep reaching for the stars". I believe Incorrect Rhymes will inspire you to use your creative minds to write amazing poems and stories.

Happy Reading and Writing!

To Elsa dream big

Janeal

CONTENTS

Ice Age

By Elma Burke

Ice Age!
You mean bondage!
No electricity
No starring at my 72 inches
Flat screen TV
Life must have been cold like ice
Without electronics
How could I survive?
Up in the air
And down on my chair
When I am playing on my XBOX
There is constant movement everywhere
It's electrifying
My heart is pumping
My brain is calculating
The pressure is so real
I can't explain how I feel
Ice Age you are wrecked!
I am now connected to the internet!

Inspiration - Some poems don't wait for pen and paper, they are created in usual places. Ice Age was birthed on the road while Janeal took the opportunity to talk about the topic he was learning at school.

Nightmare

By Janvier Burke

AAAAAAAAHHHHH
I had a nightmare
About a scary Teddy Bear
Who was giving me day care
On a very wicked punishment chair
I was dressed in my underwear
Shivering all over with fear
But at the same time
I was in mid air
I saw red gooey hair everywhere
So I declared warfare
But I could not compare
My strength to theirs
AAAAAAAAHHHHH
I need to get out of here

Tip – Find a scene for your poem then write about what you can see and how you feel.

Parents

By Janvier Burke and Janeal Burke

Parents think they have us under control
But right under their nose
We know every pose
When we are naughty
They band us from watching TV
All the praise to technology
We can record our favourite movies
We never miss a show
SHHH, let's keep it a secret
They don't really know
Parents think they have us under control
But we are the smartest beings in this world

Tip – Writing poems together with a friend or
sibling helps to build up confidence.

Poetry Crime (RAP)

By Elma Burke

It's not fair
And the Judge don't care
I did a crime
Now I have to pay the fine
I forgot to write my poetry last night
Now I am caught up in a massive fright
I tried my best, my best to explain
But all I heard was
Shame! Shame! Shame!
I got busted for a poetry crime
Now I wish I could go back in time

I had paper in my pocket
And a pen in my hand
So I pleaded to the Judge
To give me one last chance
He answered harshly with his spooky eyes
And I quickly scribble my poetry rhyme

You see, last night I went to space
Had a mission that could not wait
Earth was going to have a terrible crash
And I was not prepared to die like that
The Judge could not resist
He could not resist my rhyme
So he started tapping
To my poetry so fine

Tip - Don't be afraid to ask for another chance.
Success comes when you persevere.

Challenge 1

If you can RAP like that
Let me hear your CHAT

Write your own RAP

_____

_____

_____

_____

_____

_____

_____

_____

_____

_____

_____

_____

Money Is Funny

By Janeal Burke and Elma Burke

Money is funny
Because sometimes it goes
Dry and crummy
My favorite one is President Lumpy
I don't like Tom
Because he has a GIGANTIC tummy
Last week I bought a jar of honey
To moisturize my money
It got so sticky
The flies got really busy
I thought I would be lucky
But everything was so messy
Money is tricky
And sometimes fizzy
Money makes people dizzy
It's not funny to have money

Tip – Starting a poem and getting your Mum to finish is a great way to have family time.

I Am Bored

By Janvier Burke

I am so bored
I'm starting to be ignored
And my friends think
I am going to die of boredom
And all I can do is groan and snort
That's how bored I am
So I wrote a book of what I do
But everything is so boring

Tip - Say good to boredom forever by writing a poem explaining what you could be doing presently.

The Train Waits For Me Like A Boss

By Elma Burke

The train waits for me like a boss
I rush and leap
Trying hard not to hurt my feet
Finally, when I get through the door
My throat is cracking and sore
I can hardly catch my breath
Feels like I am in a contest
The most annoying thing
About all of this
I have to stand… no more empty seats
Oh yes!
The train waits for me like a boss
I am not sure about you
Maybe you should hop on the next bus

Warning - Never run inside the train when the door is closing! Remember you can always hop on the next train.

The Underground

By Elma Burke

People rushing, no time to stroll
The train they anxiously wait to reach
The time goes quickly
The waiting they can't bear
To get to their destination both far and near

You dear not step on peoples feet
Their faces turn scary like a beast
I must confess the underground is stress
Though the travelling time is less

The trains are parked, no space to breathe
The smell comes out, Oh Please, Oh Please
It's time to stop and the rush begins
It's never stopping, no time for ease

The underground have so much to see
The adverts you don't normally see on TV
Some people play a tune for their promotion
The underground is full of commotion

Its ups, its down, its blue, its black
The underground is full of marks
The sign gives plenty of direction
What an exciting experience
The underground

Inspiration - Pay attention to details and be inspired
by your surroundings. This poem was written
on a train to Shepherd's Bush, London.

France

By Janeal Burke

I am a tourist called Lance
This is my last chance
To visit France
I once saw pictures
Now I want to see
The real features
On top of the Eifel Tower
Living. Life. Fun.

Inspiration - A trip to France is on Janeal to do list.
Poem was inspired by hosting French students.

Challenge 2

Finish the poem France

I am a tourist called Lance
This is my last chance
To visit France

_____

_____

_____

_____

_____

_____

_____

_____

_____

_____

Tiny Bee

By Elma Burke

Don't tremble because of me
I am just a busy tiny bee
I spread pollen to grow
Your lovely spring flowers
Oh spring, Oh spring
Can't wait for your hour

Please, when you see me
Don't come near me
I am always ready to sting you
I love protecting me
Because, if I die your poor heart will cry
For my honey will no longer spread on your bread
I will vanish from this world
Without leaving a single thread

Please, don't tremble because of me
I want to be your friend
But how could that be?
When you see me again and again
Busy as a busy bee, don't stop me

Like a breath of fresh air
Spring, Oh Spring, will soon be here
Please, don't tremble when you see me
And never, never, try to collect me
I am just a busy little tiny bee
You see…

Tip - Use your spelling homework to help
you create a beautiful poem.

Poetry is Spoken Out Loud

By Elma Burke

In this house
There are poems flying all about
We hop, we dock
Our poems never flop
We dine, we rhyme
We catch them in time
We are never scared
To write down what pops in our heads
We dance, we play
We write poems our way
We laugh, we chat
We write poems to rap
In this house
There are poems flying all about
In this house
Poetry is spoken out LOUD

Inspiration - I think of my home as place rich
with poetry. Inspirations are everywhere, so I
reach out and grab the one that I need.

Caleb's Cat Scruffy

By Elma Burke

Caleb's Cat Scruffy
Was very, very naughty
He had a little coffee
With my Mummy favourite toffee
He scratched my Daddy's tummy
And stormed out the door so rudely
Caleb's Cat Scruffy
Made everyone unhappy

Inspiration - My Nephew Caleb is a very creative and lovely little boy. This poem was inspired by his curiosity.

A Pet

By Elma Burke and Janvier Burke

I am looking for a pet
That will NEVER need the vet
One that don't scratch and bark
Or ferocious like a cat

A pet that is friendly and protective
Much smarter than a detective
A pet that don't need to have a wee
And have interesting conversations with me

A pet that is tall and fast
And I can have rides on its back
I am looking for a pet
But it seems so impossible to get

Tip – Create your own imaginary pet. Write all
the features you would like it to have.

Mrs Pardon

By Elma Burke

Up in the air
David kicked the ball
ZOOOMMMMM!
It went flying
Straight into the wall
Nelly who is thin and tall
Could not stop the zooming ball
Out it went to the neighbour's garden
Ouch! Ouch!
I think it hit Mrs. Pardon
Run! Run!
We are under attack
SMACK, SMASH the ball landed
In Nelly's back

Inspiration – Janvier and Janeal always kick their football in the neighbour's back garden.

Challenge 3

Write a poem about your favourite Sport or Pet

_____

_____

_____

_____

_____

_____

_____

_____

_____

_____

_____

_____

_____

_____

I Can't Concentrate

By Elma Burke

I can't concentrate
I've been up till late
My poor eyes keeps
Blinking and blinking

I can't concentrate
I tried hard to stay awake
But my teacher keeps
Screaming and screaming

Wake up!
Wake up!
Oh no!
It's the voice of the Head Teacher
She angrily yelled
"I am calling your Mum now
And I will speak to you later"

I shouted in panic,
"Miss! Miss! I am not sleeping"
Then she proudly played
The recording of my loud snoring

The Head Teaching is watching
My heart beat is racing
I am so, so, so afraid...
My poor eyes are winking
They are shutting and shutting
I think I need first aid

I can't concentrate
I stayed up to late
Now... my Mum can't stop
Shouting and shouting

Warning – Poor concentration will prevent
you from achieving your best.

Today Was So Weird

By Elma Burke

Today was so weird
I woke up upside down in my bed
It was late
But my alarm clock showed 5am
Instead of 8
I crawled out of my bed
And twisted my leg
I cried, "Mum I am in pain"
She replied, "Son don't you dear call my name"
I could not understand
Fear covered my face
Today was so weird
I sprang out of my bed
It was only a dream
I loudly whispered to myself

Tip – Wired poems make a good read.

Challenge 4

Write a nonsense poem starting with
Today was so weird…

_____

_____

_____

_____

_____

_____

_____

_____

_____

_____

_____

_____

Impossible

By Elma Burke

It may seem too hard
To make it
It may seem too high
To reach it
When everything is against me
It looks impossible...

I never accept defeat
Because I have
The strength of a Lion
The brain of a Genius
The speed of a Cheetah
Nothing can stop me
I believe 100% in me

Tip - Believe in yourself one hundred percent (100%).

Fart Blast

By Elma Burke

My best friend Pat
Had a humongous fart
That blasted the class into space
My teacher came over
With a suit and a mask
But the smell hit her flat on her face
I had to think quickly
To bring back the kids
Soon it will be time for break
So I farted my best
And blasted Pat to meet the rest
To avoid the kids missing their break
Then in a flash
The class was back
"Oh no!" said Pat
Not another fart

Inspiration – Funny and naughty.

Sorry Sir - No Homework

By Elma Burke

Sir the reason why
I don't have my homework
When I started
My pencil broke
I looked for a sharpener
I could not find her
I had a drink on the table
It spilled all over my home work
I placed the wet homework on the radiator
Its summer no heat to dry her
Finally, I thought of a trick
But my paper was so juicy sweet
My dog started to lick
I tried to take the paper and escape
But he kept licking the juicy taste
Before I could say stop
All I heard was Gulppp!
That's was the last time
I saw my homework alive
Sorry Sir...
Next time I will
Sharpen two pencils before I start
I will drink all the juice in my glass
I will take the dog to my best friend
But most importantly
I will do my homework and not pretend

Tip - Homework is a great opportunity to
show your talent to your teacher.

Homework

By Janeal Burke

Homework is boring and steals your time

Our minds should be resting on weekends

Mummy says it good for you

Everyone knows it's too much to do

Work is tiring it makes my brain ache

Our brains should be used to solve mysteries

Raphael my brother still likes homework and the teacher

Keeps giving HOMEWORK all the time

Warning – No homework = No playtime on the weekend.

Challenge 5

Write a poem about Homework

_____

_____

_____

_____

_____

_____

_____

_____

_____

_____

_____

_____

_____

The Mess

By Elma Burke

I flipped and fluttered
And made a great cluster
Creating a complete mess
Afraid to tell my Mum
I asked my bother Tom
To help me in my distress

My brother rolled and tumbled
And everything rumbled
Making the mess disappear
But my baby sister Kasia Makayla
Burst into a terrible laughter
Causing a complete disaster

Kasia fussed and tossed
Pretending that she is the boss
Causing a smelly mess
So I rushed to her cot
But she still did not stop
GGRRR! I had no clue
What I was going to do

Inspiration – The words flip and flutter.

It's The Weekend

By Elma Burke

I jumped out of my bed
It's the weekend
It's the weekend
This tune is playing in my head

I don't have an alarm
And I tried hard to stay calm
But my belly is not impress
There is no more time to rest

Mummy in the kitchen baking away
6:30 am I am starting my day
Usually I am dragged out of bed
"Good Morning Mummy"
Is replied with nodding of head

The Xbox is on my mind
I have to win this time
There is no quiet time for Mummy
But that's not my worry, sorry

It's the weekend, It's the weekend
I will do it my way
It's the weekend, It's the weekend
On my Xbox I will play

Inspiration – The early morning breakfast
request from Janeal on the weekend.

Slippery Sliding Fun

By Janvier Burke

Ice skating is slippery sliding fun
When you are flat on your face it's not
And sometimes you feel like giving up
When you get the hang of it
The slippery slipping you cannot resist
I felt so amazed
About this man slipping
All over the place
So I tried, but I fell flat on my face
When I looked up
All I could hear was Ha-ha, Ha-ha!
Ice skating is fun
But be careful you don't fall right on your bottom

Inspiration - Janvier's first experience of ice skating.

The Dentist

By Elma Burke

I have a decay
I did not obey
I had too many
Sweetie sweets

My teeth scream loud
It needs to be pulled out
Doctor please can you come
Quick! Quick! Quick!

My mouth is upset
I feel very stress
I am not having fun
Wished I listened to my Mum

I have a decay
I did not obey
I had too many
Sweetie sweets

The Dentist is here
With his gentle care
While his needle kept smiling
At me, At me, At me

My eyes popped out of my head
Wished I was in my bed instead
AAAAHHH! STOOPPPPPP!
Can someone please help me?

Warning - Too many sweets will spoil your teeth.

The Christmas Pork

By Elma Burke

The Christmas Pork
Untied the knot
And off it ran away

It did not care
That Christmas was near
It wanted to trout another day

It ran its best
But my Uncle did not rest
He could not lose his pork

And at last
My Uncle ran fast
And tied the Pork in a double knot

Inspiration - There is no Christmas in St Lucia without pork.

Fruits Are Alive

By Janeal Burke

Fruits are alive
Watch them thrive
Fruits are alive
Can you see them?
They are walking
Through your garden
You can find them hiding
In a pot of soup
But sometimes
They are stuck in a shoot

Inspiration – Fruits.

What Wrong With Food?

By Janeal Burke

I love steak
But people call it fake

I love cake
But that is something
My Mum wouldn't bake

I am addicted to sweets
But my Mum tells me it's not good
For my teeth

I adore rice
But before I have it
I need to give my tithe

What's wrong with food?
It is something
That is really good

Inspiration – Food. What makes your favorite food special to you?

I Got A Big Scare

By Elma Burke

I got a big scare
My Teacher is here
She SCREAMMMMSS at me
And looks like a HE

I got a big scare
My Teacher is here
The clock stops the time
And my brain ditches my mind

I got a big scare
My Teacher is here
There is no playtime
To commit a good crime

I got a big scare
My Teacher is here
HELP! She is grabbing my feet
I think she is going to...

Tip – Teachers are a great source of inspiration for your poem.

Challenge 6

Write a poem describing your Teacher

_____

_____

_____

_____

_____

_____

_____

_____

_____

_____

_____

_____

_____

_____

An Average Day

By Janeal Burke

The Xbox is a console
Just like me

I make people happy
By letting them free

Sometimes I am like a bee
I sting as hard as can be

But then I calm down
And let my feelings go

I show people how I can be
Because all of that is just me

Inspiration – A reflection of Janeal's personality.

Mummy's Little Helper

By Janvier Burke

I am Mummy's little helper
As helpful as can be
Mummy says I am clumsy
But I am just being me
Mummy always tell me
She can do stuff by herself
When I really want to help
I am Mummy's little helper
As helpful as can be
Sorry I have to go
The Kitchen is on FIREEEEEE

Warning - Never put the cooker on without the permission or supervision of your parents.

Fast Asleep

By Janvier Burke

I slept perfectly in my bed
This time I was not scared
The night before
I am not sure
But all I can remember
Was curling next to my Mum like a boar
When I am afraid
She takes away my fear
Last night I slept perfectly in my bed

Tip – Overcome your fears by sharing them with your parents.

Poem Fever

By Janeal Burke and Elma Burke

My Mum has a poem fever
That never seems to leave her
She is a great Achiever
A Baker, A Poet and Bookkeeper
Her temperature was so high
I thought that she would die
I took her to the Doctor
So he could take good care of her
He said "she needs to write some more
Because a book is coming out of her"
He prescribed more pen and paper
Trying to get rid of the fever
My Mum has a poem fever
That the Doctor could not make better

Inspiration – Janeal describing his mother.

Bed

By Janeal Burke

My Uncle calls me Ted
Because I really love my bed
It's like my imagination shed
It red, white and blue
If you sleep on it
You will love it too
It goes up and down
And I mock on it
Like a clown
It's so soft it deserves a crown
I always have a frown
When my Mum asks me to get down
My bed is the best in this town

Tip – Think of things you really like and
describe them in a poem to a friend.

My Baby Boss Brother

By Elma Burke

From nowhere
The baby came here
With a vicious lovely smile
He is such a cutie sweetie pie

Mummy no longer goes to sleep
She is busy rocking all day on her feet
Daddy looks very confuse
He is suffering from late night baby blues

Everyone is constantly on attack
Baby POOHS and WEES
And also FARTS
Dust crawls all over my favourite book
And Mum forgets to even cook!

From nowhere
The baby came here
Shouting, "GOO GOO GAGA"
Mummy said, "He is the best baby brother"

Inspiration - Inspired by the movie Boss Baby.

Cup Cake

By Elma Burke

I have a confession
I never miss a special occasion
Kids go crazy
Just to taste me
I am round, small and sweet
Less than two feet
With just one bite
I hypnotize
With mouth watering flavour
You always come back for another
I dress to impress
And on a stand I shine from the rest
At your party
I keep your guess very happy
I try my best to stay to the end
But I always leave early my friend
I am your CUP CAKE
Come and get me before it is too late

Tip – Think of a riddle and write an exciting poem explaining it.

Maths

By Elma Burke

Maths is fun
Bring it on
Square root
Pie chart
I can calculate that!

2D!
3D!
Shapes in all angles
For you to see

Meters
Centimeters
Grams and Kilograms
I know length and quantity
No one can fool me

Algebra
Perpendicular lines
Maths is full of problems
I just love to solve them

Shapes and fractions
My mind is in action
Maths is a brain teaser
I can't live without her

Tip – Maths is everywhere. Practice! Practice and Practice and you will get better at it. I love Maths because it gets me to think.

Hot Chocolate

By Elma Burke

It is late
And I need to take a break
I fancy some cake
And Mummy's special hot chocolate

On the TV is a debate
About children being over weight
I called my best mate
He said, "I am having steak"

The thought of hot chocolate
Is always great
It's very late
I had to think straight

I had to compromise a great taste
To have a trim waist
I love hot chocolate and cake
But it's just too late

Inspiration – Janvier and Janeal is a great lover of Hot Chocolate.

Soldier

By Janvier Burke and Janeal Burke

I got my sword
And I got my gear
I am a soldier of God
And the devil I don't fear
My faith is my sword
My bible is my shield
I am fighting this war
And I am going to win

Inspiration – Faith.

I Have Laughter

By Janeal Burke and Elma Burke

When I am creating
I have laughter
Because my Mum calls me
A little crafter
I am super busy gluing things together
Drawing my own special characters
It always matters
When my creation shatters
Mum is a fantastic calmer
She makes everything better
Contaminates me with her laughter
And reminds me that being a crafter
Will make me happier and stronger
She says NEVER stay chatting
With failure
Look up to the CREATOR

Tip – Spending time with your Mum is very special. A hug, a kiss or one word can make a big difference to your day.

Mum At School

By Elma Burke

The day my Mum came to school
I was sweating trouble
I sat quietly in my chair
If a pin dropped
The whole class would hear

I wished so bad
That I could disappear
Everywhere I turned
My Mum was there
My Teacher, MR Mean was upset
He was pretending to be the best

My friend Super Hero Jazz
Who always wore a superman vest
Was not able to save the day
Everything seems to be perfectly okay
Then out of the blue
Kurzel took off her smelly shoes
To scratch her itchy toes
Out rushed my Mum
Escaping the STING BOOM
Ahhhh! Finally
My Mum was gone

Inspiration – How would children react if their parents came to school with them?

I Once Imagined

By Janvier Burke

I once imagined
I could be anything
A Super Hero
A Super Villon
Or a Policeman

I once Imagined
That there was a famine
And people crying
And almost dying

I once imagined
Getting secret information
Now I am older
I imagine the world
Getting better

Tip – Don't limit yourself. You can be anyone you want to be.

Challenge 7

Write a poem about your Mum

_____

_____

_____

_____

_____

_____

_____

_____

_____

_____

_____

_____

_____

_____

Mum Knows

By Elma Burke

Mum said I can't watch TV after eight
I need to eat all the food on my plate
I can't have soda
I should drink plenty of water
If I eat less sweets
I will have stronger teeth
It will keep me healthy
And I will not need
Regular visits to the GP

My friend Nola stays up late
Never eats the food on her plate
She drinks only soda
And said "it's a waste of time
to drink water"
She had so many sweets
Her mouth is empty with no more teeth
Her health is so poorly
She is always at the GP

Mum knows what is best for you
Mum Knows what you should
And shouldn't do

Tip - Follow your Mum's advice and enjoy a healthy life.

Space

By Janeal Burke

My Mum was extremely mad
And that made me very sad
I got some jelly beans
And jumped on my trampoline
I travelled into space
Wow! That's an amazing place
I got hugs from stars
And went hiking in Mars
I saw Aliens driving in little cars
Munching on Milky Way Bars
I was having so much fun
I completely forgot about my Mum
Until I heard the echo of my name
I shook my head in shame
Because I had to take the blame
For causing the flame

Tip – Take responsibility for your actions.

Introduce Yourself

By Janeal Burke

My name is Ben
I am ten
My surname is Ren
My best friend is Len

My name is Leone
I am one
I weigh less than a tone
When eating cake
I always leave crumbs

My name is Keven
I am eleven
My last name is Beven
And my puppy is called Deven

Inspiration – The name Ben.

Who Are You?

By Janvier Burke

I'm sweet
And I like to greet

I'm tough
And I play rough

I'm friendly
My Dad drives a Bentley

I'm a Teacher
I teach people about Poetry features

I'm a Dad
I'm very mad

I'm Mum
And I like helping my sons

Tip – Understanding who you are is a great way to start a poem.

Who I Am

By Janeal Burke

I'm a lawyer as good as the police
I'm a driver my engine goes VOORRMM!
I'm Zeus, I am the strongest
I'm an angel my melodies are the best
I'm a christian and I forgive
I'm a pilot that flies high in the sky
I'm a weightlifter as strong as superman
I am a king; I have great authority in my country
I am a solider that is courageous
I found out that I am creative
I can be black or white
But I am an individual
I stand out from the rest
I have discovered someone great
And his name is Jesus
And today because of Jesus we have freedom

Tip – Poems like to be read. Write yours
today and share it with a friend.

Sticks

By Janvier Burke

How can people walk in A.K.A high heels?
I call them sticks
It looks so uncomfortable
And hurt your toes
How can people walk on sticks?
Mum says it's fashionable
I think it's unbelievable
At the end of the day
They are always complaining
My feet are hurting

Inspiration – High heel shoes.

A Push And A Go

By Janeal Burke

A Push and a go
The wind is a flow
The pain goes away
You don't know
I would love to show
But you have to go
I am very sorry
You don't know
I will make one little throw
The wind is a flow
I wish I could stay
But I need to go home
Wherever I will find hope

Inspiration – Writing about feelings.

Spring

By Elma Burke

I woke up to the chirping birds
Singing the new song of the day
I no longer need the bulk of clothes
Spring is quickly coming down my way

The faces are no longer hard
The atmosphere is ecstatic
And laughter sometimes burst out loud
Spring you make everything fantastic

My eyes are open to your shinning light
My nights are getting shorter
Spring you blossom my world so bright
You such a lovely weather

Inspiration - Embracing the freedom of Spring.

Umbrella

By Elma Burke

Oops! I forget my umbrella
You again rainnnnnnnnnn!
Rain, rain, please don't come
Rain, rain, don't upset my Mum
Rain stop! I command thee
Rain stop! Have pity on me
Rain if you come
You will ruin my Mum
I will sadly have a fever
And need the scary Doctor
Definitely, I will have to stay home
Playing all day on my cell phone
You know I don't really mind
But this time, it's just not fine
Please rain, please delay
Rain stop! Come another day
Rain, rain, please don't come
Rain, rain, don't upset my Mum

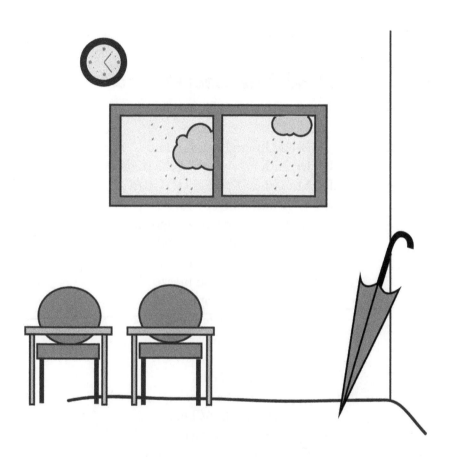

Inspiration – Unfortunately it started raining
and I forgot my umbrella at work.

Behind The Secret Door

By Janvier Burke and Elma Burke

Wow! I found a secret door
Underneath my carpet on the floor
CREAK, CRACK, CREAK, CRACK
I was not really sure
So I cracked open the door
While I ponder and ponder
WHOOSSHH the door opened wider
The gushing cold breeze
Came with a terrible sneeze
Immediately I started to wheeze
And Dad was not very please
Because He knew
I had a clue
That the door
Brought the Winter
Sorry Summer
I wish you could stay longer

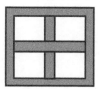

Tip - Your imagination will take you to many doors.
Open the door to discover the mystery.

Challenge 8

Write a poem about what you think is behind the secret door.

_____

_____

_____

_____

_____

_____

_____

_____

_____

_____

_____

_____

_____

Tired

By Janeal Burke

I was so tired
When I got to work
I got fired
I begged and begged
To be rehired
But my boss said
"You will never be hired"
In desperation
I got inspired
But my plan backfired
Sadly I had to retire

Inspiration - One word was enough to start a poem 'Tired'.

Rich

By Janvier Burke and Elma Burke

If I was rich
I would buy a mansion by the beach
I would travel often to Paris
To visit my buddy Harris
I would own a huarache
In every colour
And expensive clothes
Perfect for the weather
On my private jet
I would have my own exquisite chef
My favorite subjects would be
Languages and geography
Because every week I would travel
To a different country
If I was rich
I would never be stuck for a year
With the same teacher
Or often visit the office
Of the head Master
If I was rich
I would not be friends
With a snitch
I would ditch them
Super quick
Only if I was rich

Tip - Use your imagination to write about
who you want to be in the future.

The Big Red Bus

By Janeal Burke and Elma Burke

The big red bus
Drove me to Spain
And left me to walk
The big steep lane
I felt so afraid
So I quietly prayed
Then I fell sick
And needed first aid
The lady who helped
Was my friend aunty Tia
I was not happy
I needed my Mummy
At last the big red bus is here
I am very lucky
I did not have to share a tear

Inspiration - London famous Red Double Decker Bus.

Growing Up

By Elma Burke

Growing up is not for me
I am taking my time
Enjoying what the world has to see
I am not wasting time
To rush or fuss
Or day dreaming
About being the boss

Growing up is not exciting
Mummy favourite word is busy
Dad works two jobs
And still complains about money
The first alarm goes off at five
While a choir is waiting downstairs
The forks, the pans and the knives

Growing up is not in my future
When I am in bed at eight
Mummy's sore feet
Are screaming at the dirty plates
Dad is always rushing his dinner
Wishing today he could go to bed earlier
Growing up is definitely not for me!

Tip – There is no rush to get older. Make the best of each day.

Education

By Janeal Burke

The only reason you have
EDUCATION

Is to learn
INFORMATION

Mum always says have some
DEDICATION

And save the
INFORMATION

For Special
OCCASSIONS

Tip - Education is the key to success.

In My Quiet Time

By Elma Burke

In my quiet time
That is hard to find
I have a mischievous list
Of opportunities I just cannot miss

My teacher Mrs Beard
I will erase her twisted nose
The dentist Mr Peep
I will post his pictures with rotten teeth

When the school bell rings
I will get the dogs to dance and sing
And when it is time for lunch
The dinner lady will be found at the ranch

In my quiet time
There is so much on my mind
In my bedroom I will hide
Playing with my crocodile

In my quiet time
Sometimes I am really kind
And when my baby sister is restless
I dress her with my super vest

Boy Oh Boy! If she dear cries
While I am being my best
Out the window bye and bye
She will fly... goodbye

Inspiration – Janeal loves having quiet times. What is he doing?

Punishment

By Elma Burke

You can forget about Big Mac
You can forget about WhatsApp
Don't even whisper the word Subway
When we drive down the highway

Forget about Xbox
Forget about playing Roblox
You will no longer see
Spicy wings at KFC

You can forget about Football
You can forget about eating Meatballs
Forget about Pasta Bake
And having any chocolate Cup Cakes

Forget about going to Morley
Forget about getting Pocket Money
There will be no fun this Weekend
Go to bed... That's your Punishment

Tip – Obedience keeps punishment away.

Weekday Tongue Twister

By Elma Burke

Monday Makes Mental Maths Magical

Tuesday Tastes like Tasty Tango Tacos

Wednesday Weird Wind Whispers Wet Weather

Thursday Takes Trips To Turkey Town

Friday Freaks Fred's Friend Frank

Saturday Sings Strange Songs Softly

Sunday Sunny Smiles Stops Sadness

Tip - Alliteration makes your poem more interesting by creating rhythm.

Janvier

By Janvier Burke

John Judged Jan's Jam Juice

Amy Amazed Astonished Amanda

Nancy Newton knew Nelson

Vain Vanessa Vowed Victor In Venus

Inna Infinite Inspired Ivy Intelligently

Envy Ezra Excited Evadale Extremely

Revenge Roger Ran Rapidly Randomly

Janeal

By Janeal Burke

Justice Janeal Joined Jealous Joseph in Japan

Anixious Alicia Acts likes An Amateur

Naughty Nancy Named The Native Nigerians

Excited Elma Echoed EEEKKK At The Entrance

Accurate Amber Ate Apple At Assembly

Luxurious Leah Left Late for London

Challenge 9

Write Your Name Tongue Twister

_____

_____

_____

_____

_____

_____

_____

_____

_____

_____

_____

_____

The Day I Get Old

By Elma Burke

The day I get old
I will satisfy my soul
No wrinkle will cripple
No bone will become fiddle
I will sing and write
Completing many puzzles
I will dance in the rain
Jumping in muddy puddles
I will laugh and giggle
And find time to mingle
The day I get old
I will satisfy my soul
The day I get old
There will be many stories to be told

Inspiration – As I get older I would like to embrace
my creativity and enjoy life to the fullest.

My Bedtime Schedule

By Elma Burke

Before I go to sleep
I need to have another peep
So I sneak into the fridge
To have my favorite treat

I know I need to brush my teeth
But my tongue wants to lick and lick
In the dark I hide away
But Mum always finds her way

"It's time for bed, please go upstairs"
The ice cream flies from my hand
And in my fright, I had to cry
Mum! Look what you just done

Before I go to sleep
I must undress my feet
And put my socks away
Then on my knees I pray

I always waste more time
It's only eight o'clock
I'm not a little child
So I tip toe out of my room
Tick tock, tick tock

Warning - be careful what you do before bedtime
because Mums have eyes everywhere.

Mathilda

By Elma Burke, Janvier Burke and Janeal Burke

Mathilda
She is a special kind of builder
My Nan and a weight lifter

Mathilda
Wait when you see her
She is a good friend and protector

Mathilda
She lives in St. Lucia
I place I will visit in the future

Mathilda
She is full of laughter
Mathilda
Can't wait to hug her

Inspiration – Janvier and Janeal excitement
to visit their Nan in St Lucia.

Mosquito

By Elma Burke

Mosquito my friend
Do you know?
Mosquito tried to bite off my toe
I scratched and inched
I rubbed and dabbed
Mosquito bites… aaahhh is really bad
My leg swelled, the sores pained
Mosquito boy!
Trying to make me insane
I waited to see when they would attack
Mosquito jumped and bit my back
These little creates
They dangerous like a beast
Mosquito was having a British feast
I tried everything to keep them away
Mosquito was here always ready to play
I went to the Doctor
I was really scared
I told him mosquito was trying
To kill me in my bed
He starred at me with a smile on his face
And said "Mosquito, Mosquito you have to embrace".

Inspiration – Janvier's visit to the Doctor in
St. Lucia for infected Mosquito bites.

Thank You

A big thank you to everyone who read and completed the challenges.

I am excited to read all your amazing poems and comments, please send emails to elma@dejanspoetry.com

To find out more about Incorrect Rhymes workshops, events and stationery, please visit www.dejanspoetry.com

You are also welcome to email the amazing Illustrator, Ariane Motondo amaniahillustration@outlook.com or visit her website www.arianeillustration.format.com.

If you are eager to write more poems, we have included two Bonus Poems spaces to keep you writing.

Goodbye for now and thank you for making Incorrect Rhymes a success!

Bonus Poem 1

_____

_____

_____

_____

_____

_____

_____

_____

_____

_____

_____

_____

_____

_____

Bonus Poem 2

Lightning Source UK Ltd.
Milton Keynes UK
UKHW01f1534120618
324127UK00002B/230/P